Stars Dance into the Sea

Roohi Majid

Virgo Publications

Published by

Mayuri Vaid for
Virgo Publications
L-67A, Malviya Nagar, New Delhi 110017
ISBN 81-85870-44-6

Printed by

Rachna Printers
1811-A, Giani Bazar, Kotla Mubarakpur, New Delhi-110003
Mobile: 93122 40080

To my late husband Syed Hasan Majid
and to the happy life we shared

Acknowledgements

I wish to thank Dennis Evans and late Julia Casterton for their
guidance and support – leading me into poetry.

I would also like to thank my son Shahnawaz and my daughter Sarah for the warm
encouragement I have always received from them.

My special thanks to my brother Syed Shahabuddin and J.P. Das for introducing me
to Indian readers.

Contents

I

The Face of Love

Dawn

Life penetrates stillness
Liquid warmth flows.
Leaves rustle, feathers ruffle.
Honey-dew notes echo.
Breeze tiptoes among sleepy buds.
Morning glows – the face of love.

Love

Beloved,
tread gently;
I dwell more than skin deep,

in heart and mind,
feelings and perceptions,
body and soul
yours and mine.

Form and formless
full and empty;
within and without
bonded and boundless.
Love is everything,
in everything,
transient and eternal.

Life and death.
Turmoil and peace,
sound and stillness,
hurt and forgiveness,
tears and laughter—
many faces of love.

Wondrous wandering,
forever seeking,
never reaching,
as surging waves in ocean,
no beginning no ending,
flowing on, past shores of time.

In Your Absence

On a clear night
I gaze at the bluish sky,
Imagine the configuration of stars.
Flickering, in the not-so-distant past.
Telling me stories, we began
And left unfinished.

In your absence,
I keep connected with our world.
Doing the things we used to.
And things I have since learnt.
In your absence.

Now and again I allow myself,
A passing glance at life, hope, happiness
Occasionally, I catch myself laughing.
An unburdened laugh.
Surprisingly, I even indulge.
An unhurried glimpse...
Of life's little pleasures .

Moment by Moment

How tempting to watch,
My own shadow,
Conversing with silence,
Keenly sprawled, uninvited.

Rather like my cat,
Occupying the warmest spot,
On the window sill,
Above the radiator.

Void shrouds my existence
Oblivion runs through my veins.
Numbness descends.

I stare despair in the face,
Hoping it will dissolve,
In the heat of the moment,

Leaving me free,
Unburdened of memory,
Debts of my past,

Clinging to my present,
Claiming my future,
Moment by moment.

I live and I die,
Moment by moment.

Spilt Bottle

A knock, a mishap
Lapse of vision
Slip of hand.
Brush with destiny
A test of wills.
Between breaths
A pause.
A moment.

Turning around
Bottle, spilt
All that has been.
Involuntarily.
Dripping, trickling
From the edge
Of the surface.
Drop by drop
Drip by drip.

Unbonded, isolated
Aspects of life
Hopes, wishes
Aspirations.
Broken dreams
Floating streams
Of memories.
Meandering
In clear light.
Forming a formless
Puddle below.

How Much I Loved You !

Was that an act of love
or a simple goodbye;
when you said you'll never
know how much I loved you?

I'm sure I knew it before
I heard you say, then
I whispered I don't know.
Was I having a go, putting
Your feelings to test?

Maybe I just wanted
to hear it once more.
The soft-sweet confession
to warm heart, turn head.

Now it seems it's my turn
For soft-sweet confession.
I have to let you go.
I love you so.

No ceremony, no goodbye.
No clinging to memories,
rearranging pieces of the jigsaw.
rescuing moments, resketching the past.

Is this an act of love?
Is this a goodbye?
Would you ever know
how much I loved you?

The Anniversary

Holding your photograph close,
to myself, I relive the moment
of your parting, without goodbye.
Now what can I give you, my love,
that you haven't already received?
Love and good wishes, our thoughts,
linking memories, to fill our days.

The simplicity of your life, simple pleasures,
no fuss, no frills, no confusion,
Impeccable life, glad that you lived.
Gentleness and concern for others.
The healing touch, soothing of pain.
Infusing new life in withering limbs.

Strands of time have woven the years,
between us, the very stuff of our life,
which dreams are made of.
Thoughts of you turn into prayers
for Divine Light, for Eternal Bliss,
amidst Truth, Beauty, the Presence Sublime.

A life so lived, your work's done
Ours has just begun.
Life on earth is but transitory,
a privilege, a chance, an opportunity
to map out the final sojourn
to eternal abode for restless souls.

The purity of your heart and mind,
the selfless existence blossomed lives.
The fragrance that filled the yesterdays,
of all you knew, lingers in the air.
With guidance, tomorrow is yet to come.

We love you and leave you wishing
peace and joy, fairway and farewell.

The Moment

I remember the place, the hour, the moment.
Smells, sights, hush of the elements.
Mute intoxication, slow-imbibing oneness.

That silvery-gold disc, sailing
in the azure ocean of night;
our guiding star, a few paces ahead,
for comfort, pleasure and privacy.

We set sail, to unknown islands,
the enclosure of safety;
the wooden ridge, the oars, grips of your knuckles,
carving moon-passage, descending ripples.
Parting waves as loving as mother's arms.

The serenity of the Ganges
matched by the stillness of night;
punctuated by knowing, being
in the moment, alone, together.

I was ready to sail anywhere,
any number of uncharted oceans.
Halfway across the sacred river,
you turned the boat around.

Premonition hung in the air.
River flowed on.
Moon looked on.
Caravans passed.
We never made the shore.
Night sighed, stars flickered.
Moon paled, we parted.

The Last Boat

The boat moored on the Finnish Bay
of the Baltic Sea. Night interlude
for next day sails from St. Petersburg
along the river Volga and tributaries.

We made a couple of rounds
of the upper deck; the usual slow
walk after the evening meal.

Spotlessly clean, solid, bare floor
infused us with its raw energy
as each step made sole contact.

We sat on the solid iron bench
in a cosy silent togetherness; a
welcome break for sightseeing feet.

Dusk was drenched in the colour
of Volga; like the river we savoured
our moment of quiet solitude;

periodically punctuated by the
Russian Rock & Pop, drifting
out of the lounge bar.

Shall we go inside, I said, on
recognition of a sound-culture,
unfamiliar, untried by us.
I will only be tempted, you said; meant
the possibility of late drinking.

I understood, though, as usual
You didn't have the intention
or reason to say much, but we
always knew what each other meant.

Moon Masks

Face framed in charcoal lines.
Flaming against the azure canvas
your captivating smile, that rude stare.

Was that an escape from the crowd, to bathe
in the moon shower, to discover ourselves.
Our faces decked in leaves silhouette.
A picture of shifting light and shade.

Air fragrant, with jasmine, musk, queen of the night.
Wafting aroma of food, stirring of saffron, kewra.

Not too far, loud speakers were playing
love lyrics from the latest Indian movies.
We had to hold our innocent breaths.
Intense awareness of dream-desires;
a moving current, sharp and strong.

Tuned into our heartbeats, we began
singing with great passion.

★   ★   ★

Intoxicating fragrance, rose, honeysuckle.
Swirling desire abound the island of love.
Above the tops of cypresses, magnolias,
the stately moon sat radiant and content.
Following that arc of my vision, glancing words
'Lucky to have my moon next to me'.

★   ★   ★

What use, drawing the curtains,
back and forth, avoiding your gaze.
I know, you are still there, stunning,
against the indigo backdrop.
Your pale gold face, enigmatic stare
stained with joy and pain.
The malleable metal of your being
beaten into this radiant sheet.

The languishing fluidity, the trailing
brilliance of a shooting star,
visible to the lonely at night.

When the sky clears its lines,
when stars stop blinking
and the earth misses a spin or two,
the correspondence between
one and the other begins.

I hear the music of stillness.
I see your face.
I see you.

Summers Ago

Musky fragrance of summer's night,
Garlands of jasmine, beside our pillows
Through the azure canopy, studded in silver stars,
Moonbeams shimmered and showered.

Worlds afar, earth stood on its axis.
Unspoken words, the stillness.
The feel, the touch, the awakening of spirit.
Melody of a thousand ragas.

A serenade, an echo of our rhythm,
Caressing breeze, ripples in our skin.
Softly-whispering, departing night, faintly-blushing dawn.
We, alive, awake, in-tune.

II

Touch Remembers

Remembrance

Roses die too soon.
Petals fall on earth.
Fragrance lingers.
Eyes shut, colours dance.
Heart knows the rhythm.
Mind flickers.
Touch remembers.

I Remember ...

I remember you when the leafy fingers
of London plane, outside my window
touch the golden lips of the rising sun.
I remember you when the parting sun.
paints soft blushes on blue canvas.

I remember you when the birds sing
in chorus, greeting misty dawn.
I remember you when they return
to nests as dusk lines horizon.

I remember you when folds of sea
embrace swiftly crashing sunlight;
when circle within circle of memories
rise and fall with each murmur.

I remember you when I see ripples
in the lake, weaving infinitely intricate
patterns; when crushed moonlight is reflected
in the breeze, moving in and out of water.

I remember you when haunting moon
appears on grey starless mantle.
Black spots remind me of shadows
on my heart, scars of loneliness.

I remember you when night's gown
envelops the debris of my existence.
I remember you when it's you, me,
silence between, and no earthly images.

I Feel

I feel,
grief is not a dress,
worn on an occasion,
discarded at will.

I know,
Grief is the second skin
I wear, under the skin,
I had when born.

At times I notice
grazed, bruised skin
visibly lacerating wounds
Thrown to life without mercy.

At times I feel shame.
Falling from grace,
Wailing of wandering spirit.
Howling from the deepest recess.
Steaming, droplets of pain,
agony of hopelessness.

Sometimes I realise.
We have grown together.
My grief and I bonded,
grown an organic skin
to breathe and to heal.

I perceive
pain moulding my awareness
of the emerging mosaic.
Moving around, bits and pieces,
to fit in spaces.

I sense a resilience.
A wiser, kinder approach
to life, loss, pain,
urge to go on.

I hope.
When I am over the grieving,
for the love I've had,
the love I'll never have.
I'll start loving myself, others.

Love I

Let me make a chain
of love I gather as I
walk through wilderness.
Morning dew, cascading warmth,
the scent of earth, heather, pineseeds.

Love II

The vulnerability
of petal-edged love with
a heart of diamond.
Spear-sharp pangs, smeared in longing,
turn the wheel of Samsara.

Love III

Silent movement of spheres,
caresses, whispers of desires.
Awakening of the lotus;
the rainbow of hope, love, fear.
Melody burns heart; spirit whirls.

Samsara--cycle of life
death and rebirth.

Incense

An insignificant stick:
A reservoir of fragrance.

Mutating blue-grey smoke
sculptures this cylindrical vase.
Stems sprout, flowers bloom.
Fragrance gushes out; parallel
lines, occasionally intercepting.

Tender, sweet, spicy notes;
a symphony of smells.

Smoke wriggles away;
a trail of ashen leaves,
turning into nothing.

Emotions burn, unseen.
Rising and falling of breaths
dissolving in ashes,
ashes into air.

Silent witness!
Impermanence!

Meditation on a Rose

The summer you left,
roses were in abundance,
some rare blooms amongst.

I have always known
'Rose' for a symbol of love.

With loving hands you
planted 'Fragrant Cloud'.
A stunning shade of crimson,
the perfect bloom;
vibrant as first love, with
desire, to be loved, beheld.

Sun, wind, rain, frost, though
elements shaped its countenance.
It's the giving and receiving
that made it priceless.

With a touch of immortality,
in its transience, fragrance lingers
long after petals scattered around.
Beauty like yours, enters the realm
of vision forever—in another form.

I have known you, always
for a symbol of love.

Yellow

(after Pablo Neruda)

'Yellowness
Drifts from the lemon tree'
Moon looks on
Frozen in reverie.
Memory spread –
A hanging on the wall
Touched by the
Rays of your sun
Comes alive.
Your aura emanates love
I grasp joy.

Blossoms

'From the blossoms
Released
By the moonlight'
Your fragrance carried
Across.
In silence.
Moon petals lie
Breathless
On the pillows.
Silhouettes dance
On the wall.

Dreaming

Eyes wander in the depths.
Sound journeys into the silence.
Echoes fill the pit.

Withered vine, gyrating
arms grasp absent presence: you
are there, out of reach.

Fleeting feelings sweep.
Parting on the point of touch.
Smell of closeness lingers.

Flickering awareness.
Togetherness—might have been.
Touching, not touching.

I hold your love like
an emerald in my hand;
it slips as I awake.

Separate tracks: trains
passing on parallel lines.
No intersections.

Epiphany

The curved spine of Marine Drive illuminates
the cool night descending over Bombay.
Arabian Sea – breeze warm and salty.

Our family group – sister, brother, nephews, wives –
Out for a post - concert stroll before heading home.

Fresh coconut drink, roasted 'moongphalies'
Pavement trading – a welcome interlude.

Time, caught in the moment of fullness.
Life catches up with the lost rhythm.

Nothing lacks, it is complete,
just like the old times
I feel whole.

"Come on, we'are going",
knowing, you may be lingering on.
"Are you still there?," I casually ask.

Only to make sure, you aren't left behind,
I turn and I know–

You aren't on the pavement.
You aren't with us.
You are not there at all.

Feathers of Dawn

A shrine at night, winds from every direction meet,
weep and mourn under dimly awakened stars.
Frozen moon looks on.

Against silhouettes of grey houses and thinly
extending rim of the first light, strands of sun
paint blue shadows – colour of saffron.

I feel the warmth of your hand on my heart.
Dried up streams well up with longing.

Thoughts of you rise like the phoenix
From the pile of ashes and crackling wishes.

I pick up blossoms in the embers.

Something stirs the grey - pink feathers of dawn.
Morning scent instils joyful awareness.
Breeze shreds masks and layers,
tosses the cast off to the wind.

I witness trapped sun in the sky between the branches
break through.

Sparkles on dewdrops, tenderness of unfolding petals.

World reflected in morning glint.

Pain or Desire

Who has the right to eternity?
Who can claim love forever?

Underneath this ocean of bliss
there is turmoil, raging fire.

Love is walking the rope
between pain and desire.

Does the relief from pain, stem
from the absence of desire?

Is the absence of desire, the
same as relief from pain?

Does one have a say in
choosing to love or not?

Does one have a choice
between pain and desire?

Is it always either, or, in
changing states of mind?

What constant form would it
be, untouched, unchanged?

Would it open my heart,
exult my being?

Would it be as vital
as a breath of fresh air?

Would it flow as
blood in my vein?

Could it be the reason
to live, the flame, the fire?

Would it be for all seasons
from spring to winter?

Could it cross barriers
connecting earth and sky?

Could it reach galaxies
trapping moons and stars?

Could it open eternal pathways?
Could love be claimed forever?

The Unrhymed Sonnet

Desire and pain of the same organic root
Lie dormant in the depth of dark psyche.
Whatever drops, splutters, sprinkles from
Nature's fountain colours the prism of life.

Let life be generous enough to open
Its door to love, pain and desire.
Be broad enough to shoulder the cross—
The scars of living, mute absurdities.

Standing on the shore being swept away
By forceful gales or fighting back the waves.
Pushed by the debris of life, frazzled emotions;
Pulled by the urge to hold on tight, each turn.

We search every colour in the rainbow of life.
The *pearl of desire* stares from the ocean within.

Rainbow Dance

Beyond the haze of stardust, light years away
there are galaxies left behind.
A bridge of light connects their past
with my present, moment by moment.
Planet Earth spins relentlessly
charting Time's spiral motion.

We finish the instant we begin
to arrive where we left before.
Each sunrise spawns a sunset.
Each sunset scatters its glow
on the path of the rising sun.

As the light shifts through the gaps
between the blues, the greens, the browns,
renewed I arrive each morning, wrapped
in the awareness of my being.

The banishment, the sweat, the pain
in abeyance, I swing in the flux of light.
From the base of the luminous cylinder
a strand of light hits my eyes.

I see the rainbow dance.
I smell the rose of the red: the gift of love.
The blue-indigo, where the sky and sea meet:
my intuition, inspiration of life beyond.
The green earth, the fertility in harmony
with my growth, my energy.
With the wisdom and insight in
yellow-orange I reclaim Eden.
I live by the passion of crimson.
My spirit resides in violet.

The Journey

Leaving a bridge of light behind
I lean towards shadows.

Memory tiptoes between
chinks of past, present, future.
Butterfly-dance in the palm of time.

Emptiness burns slowly.
Space melts in sand.

Sea breathes in and out of me.
Waves crown, seaweed garland.

I collect silence in sound,
and cries of shells.

A string of moon rocks and
moon flakes round my neck.

I recollect shooting stars
light, furies, dazzling distances.

Separation has a jagged edge.
Loneliness cuts clean.
I descant upon the pitch of pain.

Leaving a bridge of light behind
I lean towards shadows.

When

When body feels the tremor
We tremble, tumble.

When leaves drift
Wind holds them.

When dew drops
Grass parts its lips.

When snow flakes
Earth offers its bosom.

When light sprawls
Ground spreads in front.

When stars flicker
Space embraces them.

When we tremble, tumble
Flake, flounder, fall;

Will there be someone to hold
Our mind, body, spirit?

A Wish

I wish your spirit could enter my soul;
and breathe the peace, I long to hold.
The peace in the oneness between:
the moonlight and the moon;
the music and the flute;
the fragrance and the rose.

From the centre of this sphere
to the zenith of the other,
distances shrink to dots.
The sea, the rocks, the waves:
blurred colours merge with horizon.
The radiance drapes me in desire.

Take me as I take spring breath;
taste me as I taste the sea air,
catch the foam riding high, low.

I am in the busyness of the waves;
in the blending of turquoise, indigo, blue.

Touched by the sun's gentle fingers;
caressed by the mountain air.
Grounded here, being up there.

Gifts

We have parted at the gates of change,
just as the sky drifts away from the horizon;
as the horizon moves away from the sea.

Sliding doors and spiralling images,
The giddy pace of life and its variants.
A mosaic of shades in light and dark.
Sun in mist, rainbow in the sun.

I find you quiet and easy with yourself,
now as leaves start turning inwards.
And we are still in roses and jasmine.

The crimson softness of half-moon petals
layered on tender stems bearing gifts—
fragrance, blossoms, dreams.

Here comes the challenge, the test.
The test of acceptance, as green accepts
caresses of yellow and a touch of brown.

And I learn to accept the gift of autumn;
giving in, letting go.

White Rose

In summer roses are in abundance.
Pearl- white, glistening in the light.
I remember you, the manner of your passing.
Trusting you into the arms of mother earth
to be comforted by elements only.

A solitary twig to mark your restng place.
Soon buds, blooms, ivory petals, fresh foliage.
A perfect compliment to your ivory-lilac coat.
White roses – symbol of love – bathed
in morning dew – colour of mourning.

Frost hangs upside down.
Diamond studs on emerald leaves, sleepy buds.
A few remaining petals rustle precariously.
Tears of remembrance – sorrow, relief.

With each fresh turn of the earth
concentric circles of longing decrease.
I am cleansed of the clinging to the past.
I feel fresh as rose petals in the rain.
I let go – start afresh.

Under the unfolding canopy where earth
is fragrant with thoughts of you;
you are forever in the garden of
remembrance as a pure white rose.

Rose Petals and Moonlight

Love, one star among many
In the galaxy of life.

Love could lose its innocence.
Blossoms could break the bough.

Traveller gets lost in the forest of echoes.
Fragments of desires!
Floating islands!

Wading in memories, collecting shells.
Chasing scattered rose petals,
fragrance and moonlight.

Silent interludes!

Dust may settle on panes, yet
moonlight can drip in spaces.

Shaft of joy could light the pathways;
carve out happiness in rocky terrain.

Porcelain, moonlight, rose petals.
Heart without beats, shade in mist;
lit by compassion, exudes joy.

Translucent, transparent love
infused with exuberance:
love, light, joy abound.

A bridge across shores
connects body and soul.

Love, one star among many
in the galaxy of life.

"I"

Where fragrance is not bound
By air, nor light by darkness.
Past the silhouette of night
Misty dreams of day.

Above the silvery line
Where earth meets sky.
Where waves lull the sea.
Moon casts a hazy glance.

Leaving translucent earth
Yawning, land painted in
Dawny radiance of pink
Ochre-green, peachy mauve.

Suspended in the vastness of space.
Invisible, infused, liberated.
Wings spurred, I drive my chariot;
Safe distance from the sun.

As the world sleeps, my song
Awakes celestial melody;
Piercing the blue with blues
Melting icy stillness.

Streamlined, erect, I soar
As the wish of a poet.
I touch the eternal flame;
As smoke from a candle, I
Transcend this earthly flame.

III

The World Awakes

The World Awakes
(*Patna, India*)

The shifting patterns of memories:
Juxtaposition of snaps and blots,
some preserved, some lost
in the folds of shadows.

The mirror that I hold to my
Childhood, lets me live, once more.

Brass samovar hissing away; infused
aroma of tea and fresh goat's milk.
Soft pancakes cooked the night before,
warmed up, filled with orchard honey.

Fighting sleep-dust, dusky chill,
splashing warm water gently
over face to ward off sleep.

Following prayer postures of 'Nana Abba'
we bow to our unseen God, who
we do not have the logic to doubt.

Our early breakfast done, it's
time for routine learning:
The ducks, led to the pond,
goats head towards the woods.

We are directed to our lessons
clean slates and reed pens.
We get on, the world awakes.

The Morning Out

White smock, lacy socks,
white shoes, best foot first.
A morning out, a different treat.

She carried me most of the way.
We sailed with the wind under
the bridge, through the gates.

Strange, remembering that soft touch.
My hand secure in cushioned fingers.
Her face, nor any of her features flash
but she must have charmed *amman*
to let her take me out, on her own.
The brush of her long silky hair against
my skin as she hitched me up her waist.
That closeness lingers in my nostrils.

Once inside, a grand, magical place.
Huge pillars, extended veranda washed
in sunlight, steps onto the grassy grounds.
Surrounded by trees, overarching branches
weighed down by April blossoms.

Multi-coloured cluster of children
under and around those trees;
sitting, standing, clutching their books.

Prompted by my guardian friend,
I picked up my slate and bits of chalk
to sit under the shade of a tamarind tree.
Slump seedlings dangling like balloons
from the tips of the branches.
Air warm, juicy, fragrant with nature's aroma.

52

The Pond

The tarmac road, slightly curved,
edging the vast emerald expanse.
Glass pond hand cut in the wilderness.
The sun skates in the ring of light.

Dew-soaked blue air, gleaming wetness.
Swans, ducks, ducklings follow; gliding,
bobbing in and out of water – quack –
splash – fountains of silver light, pearl drops.

Cruising towards lichen - covered
islands. Perched on the green parchment,
slender necks buried in snow-piles,
birds recall and reflect on life.

A child spellbound, treads on the
green rug, which pulls itself away.
Head down, feet up, in fast-sinking sludge,
soaked in slime from head to toe.

He surfaces, as if propelled by magic.
Water-choked and shivering, shocked;
pays silent tribute to vigilant eyes,
hands, he would not get to know.

Glass Chains

We could not, we would not
stop clawing – all fingers and nails –
for emeralds, rubies and diamonds.

Hidden treasures entangled in
the roots of the old 'Bail' tree
standing outside our house,
for as long as our memory;
generous as a sun shade,
bountiful as summer harvest.

The skill of making glass chains for decoration,
handed down, acquired, without knowing.
Searching for bits of broken glass bangles,
among grass, weeds, earth –
a prime pastime, our leisure.

The hours spent bending over
the tiny flame of the clay lamp;
watching arcs melt and shape into
many-coloured interlocking loops.

Resins of sun-drops,
streaks of rainbow,
tails of shooting stars.

Open pages of the child's book.
Illuminated.

Notes of the manuscript
preserved.

You and I

I have watched over you,
seen you glow with life, love,
melt with tenderness.
I have witnessed your loss, pain.
A life, bereft, strained.

I feel you live in me, I in you...
You take my breath away.
I breathe for you, you for me.
I see with your eyes;
feel from your heart.
My breath mingles with your sigh.
I wipe your tears, share your smile.
My arms cradle you in swaying breeze.
My presence comforts you in moments of need.

Rings on my flesh,
ripples in your skin.
Folds of our consciousness
mark the hands of time...

I have caught a glimpse of your face
gleaming in gentle morning light.
You have sensed my presence
behind frost-laced glass curtains.

Often, I felt your wish to hide inside me.
A shelter in my tent – from wind, rain, sun.
The light filtered through my canopy,
brought warmth and comfort to you.

My sap, my life-blood runs in your veins.
Each tendril, every shoot and bud
in tune with the rhythm of your mind.

You and I live together, grow together;
come and go in this cycle of creation.
Grounded in the life-source.
I, in this soil, you on your patch of earth.

On Hampstead Heath

Morning washes off the early mist,
grass still and moist with night's tears
Heath awakes to birds, joggers and dog-walkers.
Fresh morning scent permeates the air
The magic of silence lures me.

Drifting amongst low bushes in the clearing,
my feet sense the comfort of a grassy patch,
hidden between trees under the blue canopy,
patterned by the arching branches.

High above the sun radiates diamond sparks
and cuts the glassy sheet of air.
Leaves bathe in genle amber light.

My eyes glimpse the autumn mosaic
yellow, green, rust and brown –
the burning bush on the ground.

Drenched in the ethereal warmth;
muted, in awe and wonder
centred, between earth and sky,
rooted deep into the ground
held up by heavenly thread.

Stilled at heart and mind,
I take the breath of life.
Touched by the Infinite,
Peace becomes me.

On the Island

Night !
Dark, silent!
Comforting!

Black ink spilt on ebony slab.
Non-visible patterns.
Sounds merge.
Forms unbounded.
Memory – statuettes, shadows, silhouettes.
I am safe in this magic cloak.

Hazy star-beams.
Light piercing the skin of earth between me and heavens.
A billion light years away life breathes.
Echoes!

This planned escape– a calculated alienation.
An arranged samsara.
This yearning for rebirth as a mythical bird of paradise.

The craving for the fire and fury!
Do I need to be engulfed by flames, always?
Am I destined to be turned into ashes before I can fly?
Or am I just waiting to be rescued from the preordained?
Wishing the tides of the mundane swept away.

Left on the moon-sickle of Corfu I imagine
the clearest view of the islands in the Ionian Sea.
Surrounding the mountain range of Kerkyra, the sea,
the waves, the rocks are ever present.

The isolated grandeur of night blends with pine bends
and olive groves of the day, carving crescent bays.
Islands within islands.
Earth and water softened in air, colour, light.
Lush green dressing of pale saffron land!

This luscious island!
Is this my Eden?

Revisit

I hear the cicada's piercing cries.
Birds are cheeping and chirping.
Dogs lie low, cats busy grooming.
My energy ebbs and flows in stillness.

Hedge-men camouflage around
the enclosure – watch and wait.
Who are they keeping out? What
secrets between this green and blue?

The date palm towering over my
shelter, lit by fireflies in darkening
nights. A home from home always,
here in my chosen exile.

Pink-white honeysuckle, guiding
stars at nights – the wafting
aroma mingles with grass, shrubs,
earthenware pots and stones.

Sun rays behind the yellow curtains
knock gently at the glass pane
precisely, the moment I wish...
a warm greeting.

Eyes, ears – flickers of the mind at work.
Heart's melody un-picks the past-present. Mapping
what I create as needs, what's received as gifts.
That *then*, this *now*, been within me, always.

Creation

I do not know if you saw a
candle lit, deep in my soul.
I could see God smile in your face.
That moment of bliss, suspended in
eternity–bonding with Infinity.

Overwhelmed by the generosity
Of God, man, nature, we looked on.

'Put it in your category of–-'
'Gifts', I comprehend and complete.

A last minute decision to sample
Aeschylus: Myth, Tragedy, Images
A metaphor for Creation, perhaps.

Minutes later, cheese on toast
sizzles deliciously, bubbling as a lunar
landscape millions of years ago.

Golden crust matches the anticipation
and shapes into a grin, mingling
with the aroma of loving concern.

A far cry from the labours of
Hercules or the passions of
Furies I am about to discover.

Cinder

A bunch of freesia slowly drying,
Sitting pretty on slender stems.
Saffron wings hanging upside down.
I smell buttercups in the air layered with echoes.

Memory replays the dramatic entrance
to the Royal Festival Hall.
A brolly and a bunch of flowers,
a few fugitive droplets on your forehead.

Today on my way back from work,
I almost bought an identical bunch.
Acquiring a replica seems like forgery.
Could it have your signature
smile, warmth of your fingers
as they touched mine?
Can fantasy turn cinder to flame?
Can fire bloom?

Untitled

We walk on yellow carpet.
Breeze spurs us on.

Clusters of clover swing drunk.
Buttercups dance in circles.

We could hear the grass speak.

Absorbed in abundance,
we lay in nature's cradle.
Silence is nourishing.

Bearded men of grass guard the land.

Overhead floating islands
regroup in strange shapes.

Wrapped in muslin warmth,
suspended between 'now' and 'then'
Present stands forever.

Nature follows its course.
Earth turns on its axis.
Sun's on its way out.

Will there always be light
And warmth and silence
to nourish us?

Silence

Water spanned receding light.
Speckled blue canopy above
Quiet waves below.

Fusion of light, water, air.
Moon-fluid spread
To the edge of saffron sand.

I stood, transfigured
Overwhelmed by the generosity
Of the elements.

Sequenced cloak laid at my feet,
Cleansed with bubbling milk.
Spirit imbibed tenderness.

Breeze murmured, mingled
With heartbeat tingling
With the awareness:

Alone!
Infinite Space!
Silence!

The Orchard

Once nestled among mango trees
now teak saplings guard the tomb.
Crystal light flows through leaves.
Butterflies flutter by.
Cluster of yellows, whites sway:
confetti to welcome the spring.

This lush green exuberance
the presence I sense here.
This scent I'll know anywhere.

Past sails under the forgotten arches.
Memories span days, years.
Bridges and bonds—
daughter, father, man.

A life self-sustaining, giving.
A heart endowed with resins of love.
Deeds, intents rooted in compassion
blossom, bear many hopes, joys.
Slender stem crowned with pure-white
lotus rises above the murky soil:
spirit triumphs over body.

Between sunrise and sunset
perpetual spring reigns.
I breathe the earth
my father sleeps in.

If Only ....

Must admit, I have stepped over
the mark accusing you of forsaking
us when we need you most.
But surely you are aware of this.

The voice keeps buzzing –"pull yourself
together". And I want to scream.
It's your world not mine; you control
lives, deaths and everything in between.

I claim no power over the fate of a clay
pot. Imagine shattering without a slip
or a shudder, at the mere touch of my
fingers, such beauty and colour into bits.

Forgive me, if it's a sign or a warning
I don't get it now, nor did I then.
An interrupted siren jammed the air
waves trying to reach my ears.

"Look at her composure".
"She didn't even swear".
"Oh well you could have lost your legs"
(a sympathetic onlooker)

Submerged in that moment, surfacing
at last. I hear – "It could have been my life".
(clearly my voice)

That moment, unknown to me,
thousands of miles between us,
'you', my mother, you are going into
cardiac-arrest – never to return
to my life, my world.
If only...

How Would I Go!

I go with memories.
A whiff of fresh air.
A glance, a smile
Soft syllables, listening ears.

How would I go!
I go with the touch to remember.
Fragrance that lingers.
I part – amongst family and friends.

How would I go!
I go on the wings of love.
The arrow of the moment points
To peace – sublime and eternal.

Notes and Memories

I carry your photograph with
Juliette's snaps, wherever I go.
The present arises from the past.
Blue mist peeps out of every
Chink and fold in the present.

Units of past-present make up
The continuum of time in
This space, we define as life.
And the art of living is the
Composition of notes and dreams.

It may appear linear as we
Consider the gains and losses.
What's out of sight, often turns up
At the next round, though least
Expected, often forgotten.

Surface glaze may mask the faces
Behind fragments and creases.
Days and years click back
Into beginnings and endings.
Yesterdays become todays.

Ganga Ghats at Varanasi

(*Steps on the bank of the Ganges*)

Majestic Ganga, eternal, boundless!
Graceful, serene, effortless flow!

Floating silhouettes on water.
Wind flirting with light in sunshade.
High above the steps, beyond the skyline
the rampart of the ancient fort, temples, buildings
Sun-god gives the last 'Darshan' of the day.
Glorious mandarin disc, suspended in horizon
shedding its multi-layered garment for a dip
in holy water, just as many thousands of devotees
would, on 'Makar Sankranti,' this Spring.
A ritual ablution, performed by Sun-god, as retiring
behind the western rim, gateway to heavens.

Saffron dust sprinkled in air to welcome Ganga-mata
dressed in shimmering peachy folds of water.
Infused with warmth, air bubbles emboss
self-perpetuating ripples on the surface.

The long narrow boat, three occupants, mute spell
the vastness, the grandeur of Ganga and the clay
deepa, traded by the little girl with a smile and
amazing bargaining skill, for a few rupees, bravely
sets off, on its leafy raft to uncharted waters.
The flickering light, faintly glowing halo, a symbol
of hope, confronting darkness and uncertainty.

At dusk, in January, Ganga – too cold for a cuddle;
I can only caress the lightness of your being.
Let your moist softness run over me;
your 'Amrit Dhara' drip through my fingers;
your ethereal essence embalm me.
Your sacred channel connects me with all that
you symbolise – the enigma, the challenge, the quest

the eternal flow of life; the journey of a mere trickle
from godly abode, in the Himalayas across the
the Gangetic plains, nourishing body and soul.

Your homage to Sun-god, commemorated
as 'Surya Namaskar' each day at sunrise.
Offerings of Gangajal and milk, sprinkled
with rose petals, saffron, sandalwood.
Garlands of marigolds and jasmines.
Air purified with butter, burning incense, perfume.
Reverberated chants, mantras, cymbals, gongs.

The moment is suspended in time, plaited in strands
of belief – awe, wonder, love and devotion.
I submit myself to the memory of such moments
when earthly existence transcends, melts into
eternity – no beginning, no end, no want, no pain.

'Santosh' resides;
Spirit at peace;
A metamorphosis!
Echoes of creation!
Primordial melody!
Song of the universe!

Aum Shanti
Shanti Shanti
Silence!

References

Ghats – banks
Darshan – audience,
Makar Sankranti – Spring festival of fertility and harvest
Surya Namaskar – salute to the sun
Amrit Dhara – nectar
Gangajal – holy water
Santosh – bliss
Aum – Primordial vibration
Shanti – peace

Haiku on Light

Saffron specks flood in.
Glass-panes, nets hold sun and fire.
I breathe colour and light.

Pearly sheen settles.
Interface of crystal light.
Herring-bone imprints.

Pure, virgin water
lulled by perpetual motion
spins a rainbow yarn.

Fountain drops break off.
Liquid leaves scatter on grass.
Reincarnation.

IV

Stars Dance into the Sea

Stars Dance into the Sea

From the jetty the sea appears mild.
The sandy hemline of the wavy garment
elegantly embroidered in milk-bubbles.
Darts of light target the grey canvas, stretched above.
Jumbled up clouds saunter away, carefree.

All I wish for is the sun.
And it comes—the midday sun appears
with a vengeance; thrusting bright orange
spears in every direction.

From each of the diamond points, fire drops
roll down the cheek, the bosom of the air,
rolling right down into the lapping waves.
All around me whirling stars... falling into the sea.

Diamond and jades float-dance on wavy rafts.
The blue-turquoise calm turns into a dazzling
fire-breathing dance...

Caravans of fireflies on their way back
bridge the sky, the air, the sea.
Perhaps this is the way the sea remembers its dead.
Floating candles – yellow, blue, green, white.

The parting gift – the energy of the split atoms of the sun.
Ashes turn to flames.
Stars dance into the sea.

Explosion

A distant star explodes
setting life sparks flying.
Atoms of creativity in orbit.

The 'Beginning'

Electrons of colour in human form
whirling, oscillating,
breathing, balancing
arms, limbs, torso.

Symphony of movement.

Languid curves, arabesques
intertwining with dedication
effortless precision.

Reverberation of cosmic footwork.

Profusion of hues, spiral of rainbows.
Sparkling trails—rhapsody of motion.
Weaving pulsating harmony.

Resonating eternal melody.

Fluidity, lightness of vibrations.
Luminous transparency of
butterfly-wings, flitting in unison.

Life, love, intoxication.

As if Radha and gopis,
after the ritual dip in the river,
are drying colour-soaked saris.

Krishna, the love-god
eyes and smiles.

Love, life, devotion.

Surya Namaskar

(*Salute to the Sun*)

Footprints and fragrance
smudges of peach and honey
on ash-blue canvas.

Dawn trails across this unsustainable expanse...

Unlocking pale grey gates
of horizon, the sun edges
out, inch by inch.

Flustered fuchsia-face, quivering, struggles to pop out.

Cherry blossom streaks,
Smears on its soft-warm face
Belly expanded with in-breaths.

Mingled with the fire-flux of the receding dawn –

splinters and darts blown over
the four corners of mute space
before assembling as segments.

A third, a half, then three quarters swiftly come together.

Unblemished pink-orange
face of the sun sails
across the rippling yarn.

Framed within the leaves and branches of the trees

right above where I stand
I can feel its breath close
to mine, steeped in warmth.

Muscles and body toned, I take my place in the scheme of the day

I offer Surya Namaskar.

The Last Rites

At the end of the day, chores
out of the way, the sun casually
slings oars over its shoulders.

Propelled across the dusty glow,
chanced incisions emboss the ash-blue
canopy with the remainder of light.

Some distance from the source
unconcerned, perhaps indifferent,
sparkles flicker in the haze of clouds.

Raw energy uncoils as the serpent
of dusk slithers in empty spaces,
breathing fire into mute forms.

Turquoise sea soaks up the zest.
Peach sky weaves into apricot waves.
Azure patches shimmer in sand-grain-light.

Soon, an ebony disc resting on a pyre
of saffron flames diminishing sky-land mass.
The sea simmers down to dots and dashes.

Pale sun-bird perched on this grey mast
takes off in the heat of silence. Gravity
leaves me stuck to the burial ground.

Samudra Beach

(Kerala, South India)

Waves barely touching my toes recede
like dream-desires, unsubstantial, unfulfilled.

All that energy dissipated in the breeze between
the turquoise Arabian Sea and the ash-blue sky.

Upright, ankle-deep in the golden sand,
I wait, wait for my chance to mingle
toes with the sea, sun and tidal waves.

Next, the unexpected surge of Poseidon force.
A glass-green wall — waves as high as surrounding
hills come crashing on the sand-field.

I stand, transfigured, just feet away till
the swirling mica rolls back into the sea.
Milk-bubbles wash my feet.

Here I am, left with sun grains between
my toes and sea on my face.

Renewal

As sunrise and sunset weave
an infinite loop, winter gives way
to spring; summer, autumn follow on.

Leaves fall ensuring budding.
Seeds smell of blossoms, spawn colour.
Where grass is trampled, wild flowers grow.
When earth recedes, rivers, oceans flow.

A thousand stars weep, as dawn breaks.
Across the sky, strident moon bows
to sun in trails of silver dust.

Peach-crimson shadows cast on rippling yarn.
Petal-soft caresses of scented breeze;
Rocks lapping waves, pebbles washed ashore.
Symphony of sight, touch, sound.

Warm-soft hand to hold, arms around.
Watching birds, feeding ducks.
Smell of fresh blossoms, ice creams:
Past silhouette of time–born again.

Grief, pain bring nourishing rain.
Every colour in the rainbow–a mirror of life.
Each image – an enduring tale.
A renewal – Love after love.

A Miracle of Life

(for Seebra Meera)

God's gift
Miracle of life
Breath of fresh air
Meadows, spring flowers
Blossoms everywhere.

Almost perfection
Each and every detail
Down to finger nails.
Pink-white skin
Petal-soft lips
Black-silk mop.
Hazel-brown eyes
Opening, closing
Wondering, wandering
Smiling, talking eyes.

Demand for feed
Simply, attention
Hold, touch.
Comfort of a lap
Familiar smell
Mother's breast
Fountain of life.

Fisting, stretching
Effort, perseverance.
Aware of your place
Your beauty, charm
Inner strength
Purpose in life.
Go hand in hand
With love and peace.

A Wedding Wish

(for Shahnu and Konni)

Marriages are made in heaven,
We used to say, but what of those
Who do not entertain God or Heaven.
No doubt, you too, will create
Your own heaven, a sanctuary
Of love, trust, happiness.

Your search for *'the ultimate reality'*,
The mystery and wonder of life,
Long may it continue!
Quantifying the unquantifiable.

The kernel of existence, in
All living forms, is *Love*
The force, the movement creates
A pathway of energy, connecting
The material to the spiritual.

The certainty that rarely comes
In life, suddenly you know is here.
The moment to sip the wine
From the goblet of *Love* has arrived.

I wish you too, love and contentment
At heart, health and happiness.
Fusion of spirit, body and mind.
May your creativity blossom with humanity!

With love and best wishes to *Shahnu*
And *Konni* from one in person, the
Other in spirit, beyond physical confine.

When You Smile

(for Juliette Majid)

You only have to smile, once.
Golden drops rain down.
Blue diamonds sparkle.
The room is lit.

Rays from your eyes hit the chandelier.
Strands of light... streaming down.
Rainbow on the walls and ceiling.
Love, light, colour – A perfect harmony.

When you smile.

Khurram

I named you after
a Mughal prince.
Your persona befits it.
Your passion matches
the legendary love
that lives forever
in the echoes of Taj Mahal
that Shah Jahan built
for Mumtaz Mahal.

Your eyes change
when you look at me.
Warm mellow gaze
drips honey.
Serene blue vastness
tapers to a red flame.
Black dot quivers
emitting sparks.
Dancing stars
in the pool of calmness.
I am drowned!

Body flung at my feet.
Toes licked wet.
Downy chin raised for a caress.
Love the way you place it
in the cup of my hand.
Total trust, unambiguous
unconditional.

Tail curled in, retracted claws.
Pearly pink paws.
Satin touch.
The privilege of stroking
your velvet belly!

The contour of your face:
a silent witness of devotion.
Softly rising–falling breath;
murmuring breeze
whispers that which
I know too well.

Inside your furry shell
you transform into
a composite purr...
alive, content – Khurram.

Mother India

(On the 55th anniversary of Mahatma Gandhi's assassination)

This upsurge of blood and fire.
Volcanoes of communal strife
Has *Odysseus* really reached *Ithaca,*
Or is it *Ithaca* that's no longer there?

Where is the place, the narrow dusty
lanes edging farms and fields?
Lakes and brooks along hills and glens?

Eye of the sun stares at murky,
bloody water. Light-fragments
zipped in breeze are no diamonds.

Where is the bustling market, patchwork
crowd? Stalls of fruits and flowers, scented
garlands for *puja* and calls of *muezzin?*

And wild growth along hidden pathways,
leading to pastures where sheep grazed.
Our bit of Eden is there no more.

The excitement of picking marigold
magnolia, jasmine and basil to scatter
At *Saraswati's* feet – the goddess of the Arts.

Where is the land I left decades ago
with the custodians of Ganga and Jamuna
in Gandhi's India? Who is guarding
the love and honour of Mother India?

Muezzin—One who calls Muslims to prayers
Ganga and Jamuna, the two rivers, symbolising
Hindu and Muslim communities in India.

Night Covers All

Gaps between the roads and the rubble.
Grand houses, flats touching the clouds.
Lush spaces between ochre patches.

Moon hangs low – pale, boat-shaped.
Silver dust pumps up air vents.
Cows, dogs, men huddle on roadsides.

Financial reservoirs aglow.
Enflamed passion, calculated aspirations.
Night-day plots, fresh killings.

Sleep-sparklers on *kholi* windows.
Welcome night – new dreams
Night covers all.

Roohi Majid's poems take us from a profound love of the earth – her creatures, her trees, her incredible sunsets and weather – into meditations on ourselves in relation to the gods, the cosmos, and one another. She is a poet of political love and commitment, she is intensely personal, and she is also at home in the realm of the abstractions. In short, her country is everywhere.

Julia Casterton
(Poet. Teacher. Tutor. 2003)

From the City Literary Institute, London

'Roohi Majid's poetry reflects the two cultures
to which she belongs. That of India, and of Britain.
She has the ability to write on subjects ranging
from the everyday to the metaphysical'.

Dennis Evans, Tutor.
The East Finchley Poetry Writing
Workshops, London

Roohi Hasan Majid

Roohi Majid, teacher, poet and translator has a Doctorate in Literature from Patna University in India and a Masters degree in Education from the University of London.
Roohi has studied poetry at the City Literary Institute, L.U. Institute of English and attended workshops in Finchley, Arvon Foundation and Poetry School Venues in Britain and Abroad.
She writes mainly in English, also in Urdu and translates to and from English, Hindi and Urdu. Roohi is widely published in U.K. and India. She has contributed to magazines and anthologies, some of which are mentioned below:-

- The Redbeck Anthology of South Asian Poetry U.K.
- Reflections: An Anthology of Mystical Poetry U.K.
- Human Tide and Tears of Plenty-The Camden Poetry Group
- Online Archive of Poetry Magazines. The Poetry Library, London
- Equinox
- Fire
- Reflections
- Indian Literature: Sahitya Akademi Journal India
- Aaj-Kal New Delhi

Some of the poems included in the book have appeared first in the above publications.

Academic Work:

"Fazal Haque Azad, His Life and Works" (Doctorate in Literature) Book published in India (1982)
MA Ed Dissertation (1986) 'Commonwealth Population in Britain".

Occasional Papers: Literary, Socio-cultural and Educational.

Roohi Majid has worked jointly on "The Translation Project" (English to Urdu) with Dennis Evans, a well-known contemporary English poet.